# HAL•LEONARD
# GUITAR PLAY-ALONG®

# VAN HALEN
## 1978-1984

## VOL. 50

Cover photo: © Neil Zlozower/ATLASICONS.COM

ISBN 978-1-4768-7447-0

# HAL•LEONARD®
# CORPORATION
7777 W. BLUEMOUND RD. P.O. BOX 13819 MILWAUKEE, WI 53213

In Australia Contact:
**Hal Leonard Australia Pty. Ltd.**
4 Lentara Court
Cheltenham, Victoria, 3192 Australia
Email: ausadmin@halleonard.com.au

Visit Hal Leonard Online at
**www.halleonard.com**

# Guitar Notation Legend

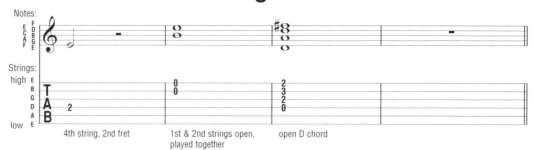

**THE MUSICAL STAFF** shows pitches and rhythms and is divided by bar lines into measures. Pitches are named after the first seven letters of the alphabet.

**TABLATURE** graphically represents the guitar fingerboard. Each horizontal line represents a string, and each number represents a fret.

Notes:

Strings:
high E
B
G
D
A
low E

4th string, 2nd fret · 1st & 2nd strings open, played together · open D chord

---

**HALF-STEP BEND:** Strike the note and bend up 1/2 step.

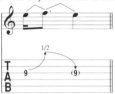

**WHOLE-STEP BEND:** Strike the note and bend up one step.

**GRACE NOTE BEND:** Strike the note and immediately bend up as indicated.

**SLIGHT (MICROTONE) BEND:** Strike the note and bend up 1/4 step.

---

**BEND AND RELEASE:** Strike the note and bend up as indicated, then release back to the original note. Only the first note is struck.

**PRE-BEND:** Bend the note as indicated, then strike it.

**VIBRATO:** The string is vibrated by rapidly bending and releasing the note with the fretting hand.

**PALM MUTING:** The note is partially muted by the pick hand lightly touching the string(s) just before the bridge.

---

**HAMMER-ON:** Strike the first (lower) note with one finger, then sound the higher note (on the same string) with another finger by fretting it without picking.

**PULL-OFF:** Place both fingers on the notes to be sounded. Strike the first note and without picking, pull the finger off to sound the second (lower) note.

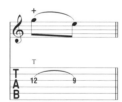

**LEGATO SLIDE:** Strike the first note and then slide the same fret-hand finger up or down to the second note. The second note is not struck.

**SHIFT SLIDE:** Same as legato slide, except the second note is struck.

---

**TRILL:** Very rapidly alternate between the notes indicated by continuously hammering on and pulling off.

**TAPPING:** Hammer ("tap") the fret indicated with the pick-hand index or middle finger and pull off to the note fretted by the fret hand.

**NATURAL HARMONIC:** Strike the note while the fret-hand lightly touches the string directly over the fret indicated.

**PINCH HARMONIC:** The note is fretted normally and a harmonic is produced by adding the edge of the thumb or the tip of the index finger of the pick hand to the normal pick attack.

---

**TREMOLO PICKING:** The note is picked as rapidly and continuously as possible.

**VIBRATO BAR DIVE AND RETURN:** The pitch of the note or chord is dropped a specified number of steps (in rhythm), then returned to the original pitch.

**VIBRATO BAR SCOOP:** Depress the bar just before striking the note, then quickly release the bar.

**VIBRATO BAR DIP:** Strike the note and then immediately drop a specified number of steps, then release back to the original pitch.

---

# Additional Musical Definitions

*(accent)* · Accentuate note (play it louder).

*(staccato)* · Play the note short.

**D.S. al Coda** · Go back to the sign ( 𝄋 ), then play until the measure marked "*To Coda*," then skip to the section labelled "**Coda**."

**D.C. al Fine** · Go back to the beginning of the song and play until the measure marked "*Fine*" (end).

**Fill** · Label used to identify a brief melodic figure which is to be inserted into the arrangement.

**N.C.** · Harmony is implied.

 · Repeat measures between signs.

 · When a repeated section has different endings, play the first ending only the first time and the second ending only the second time.

# VAN HALEN
## 1978-1984

**VOL. 50**

# CONTENTS

# Ain't Talkin' 'Bout Love

**Words and Music by Edward Van Halen, Alex Van Halen, Michael Anthony and David Lee Roth**

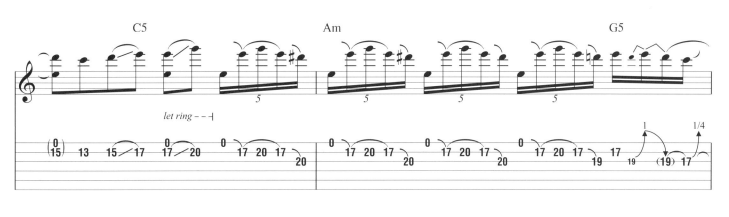

**Chorus**

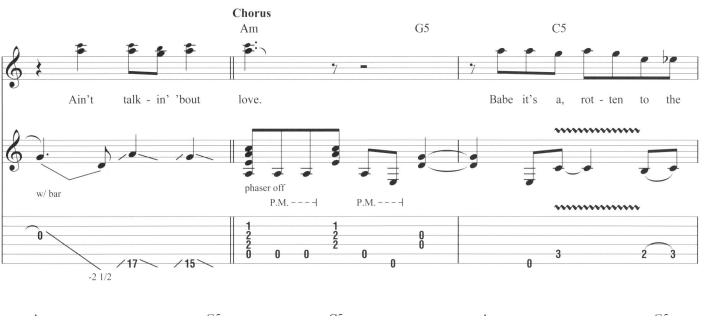

Ain't talk-in' 'bout love. Babe it's a, rot-ten to the

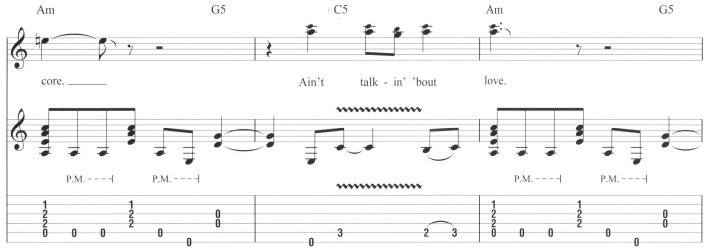

core. Ain't talk-in' 'bout love.

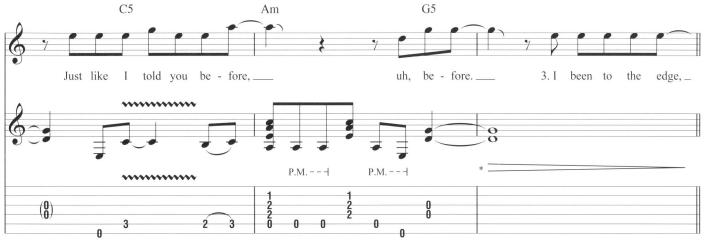

Just like I told you be-fore, uh, be-fore. 3. I been to the edge,

*Decrease vol. knob to 1/3 volume.

*Additional Lyrics*

2. You know you're semi-good-lookin',
   And on the streets again.
   Oo, yeah, you think you're really cookin', baby.
   You better find yourself a friend, my friend.

# Beautiful Girls

**Words and Music by Edward Van Halen, Alex Van Halen, Michael Anthony and David Lee Roth**

Tune down 1/2 step:
(low to high) Eb-Ab-Db-Gb-Bb-Eb

1. She was a

**Verse**

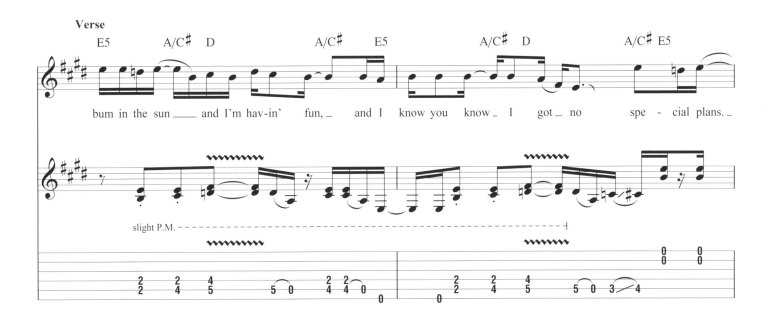

bum in the sun ____ and I'm hav-in' fun, _ and I know you know _ I got _ no spe - cial plans. _

_____ (Spe - cial plans.) _ All the

bills are paid, _ I got it made in the shade and all ____ I n - nee-need _ is _____ the

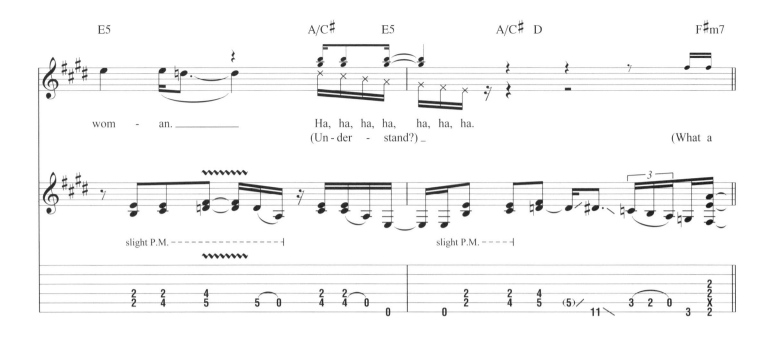

wom - an. _____ Ha, ha, ha, ha, ha, ha, ha.
(Un - der - stand?) _                                    (What a

**Pre-Chorus**

sweet talk-in' hon-ey with a lit-tle bit o' mon-ey, she turn ___ your head a - round.) _

A crea-ture

from the sea ___ with the looks to me ___ like she'd like to fool a - round. __

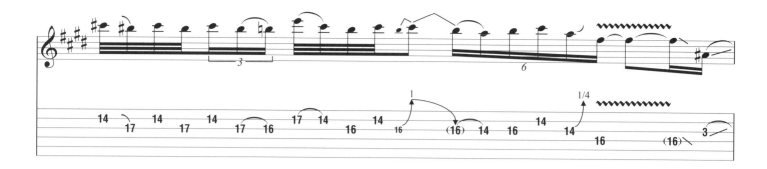

**Interlude**

*Spoken: Sit down right here.*

*Oo,        la,        la!*

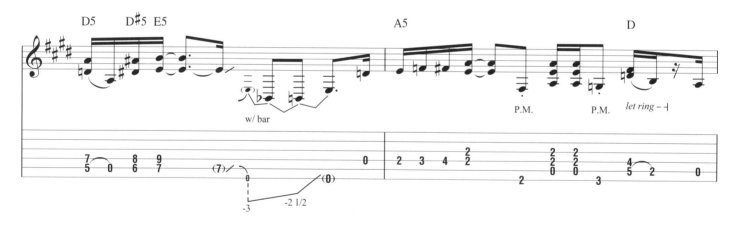

*I think I got it now.*

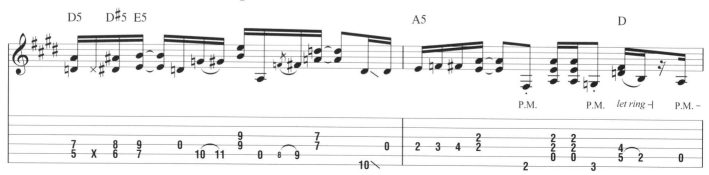

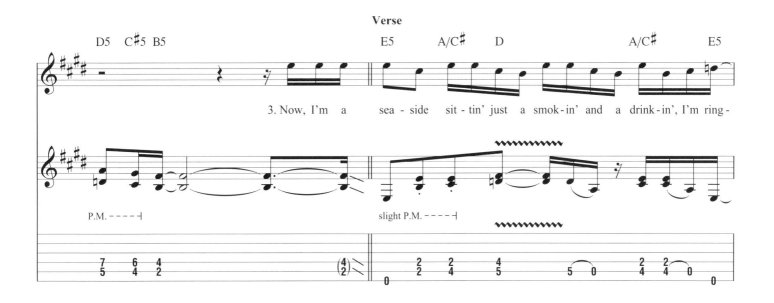

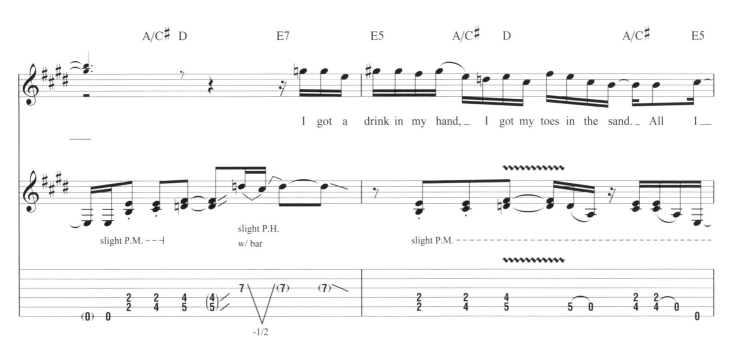

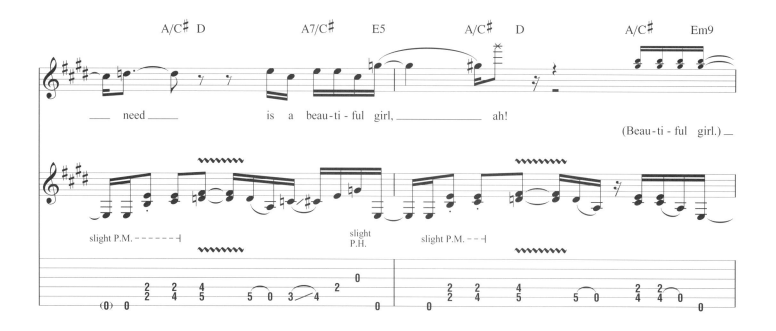

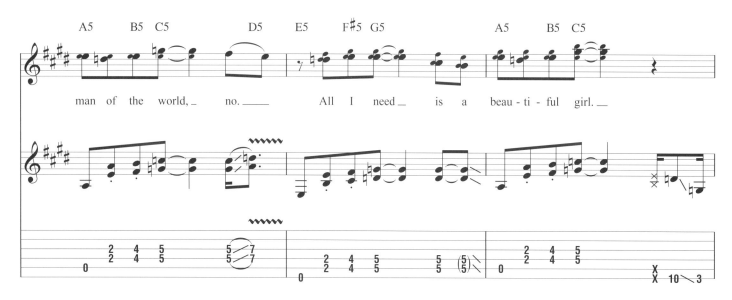

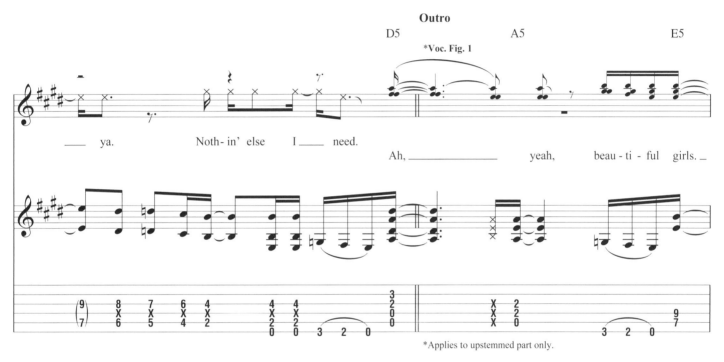

*Applies to upstemmed part only.

Bkgd. Voc.: w/ Voc. Fig. 1 (8 1/2 times)

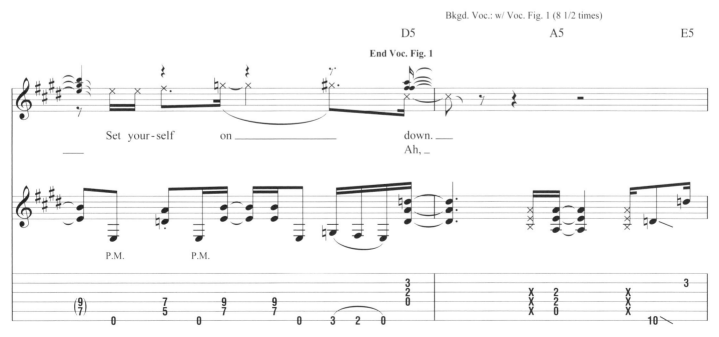

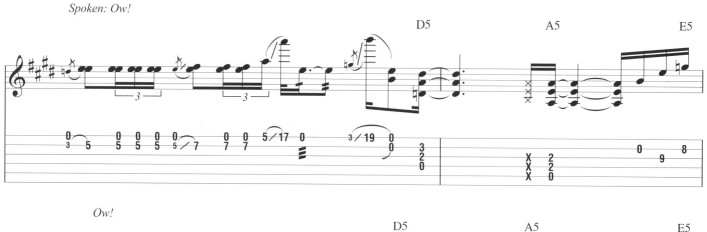

*Ow!*

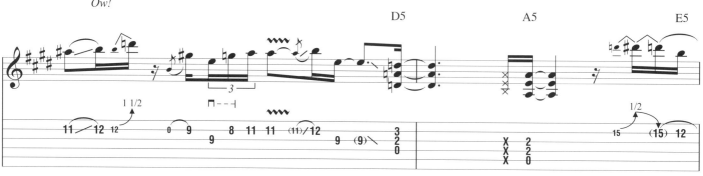

*Woo!*     *Come here, baby. Come here.*          *Yeah.*

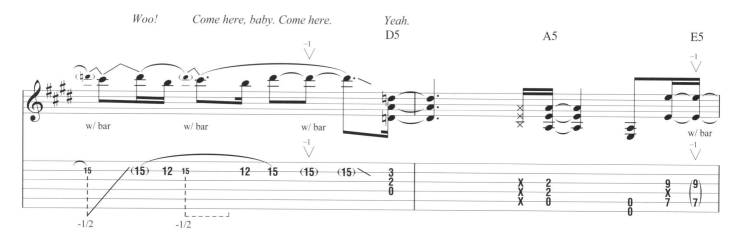

*What's your name, honey? What's your... Hey,     hey,  where you goin'?   Hey!*          *Hey!*

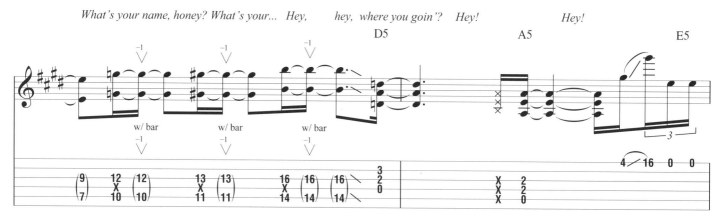

*Hey,  babe, wait.*                    *Oh!*

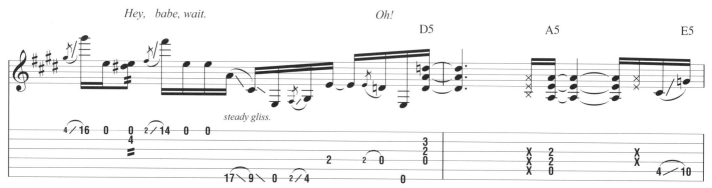

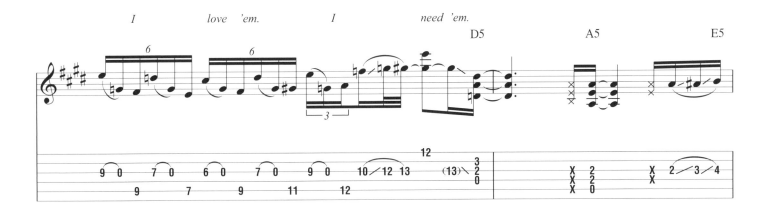

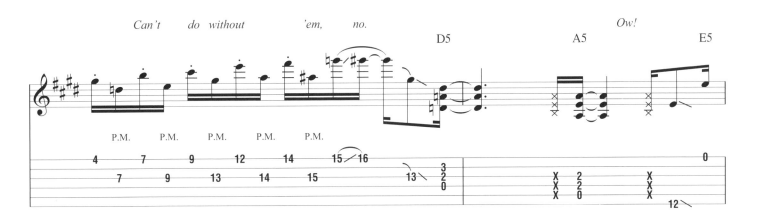

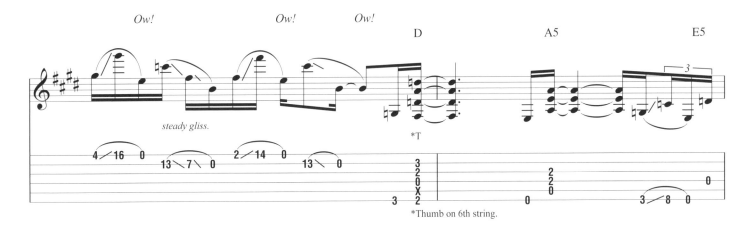

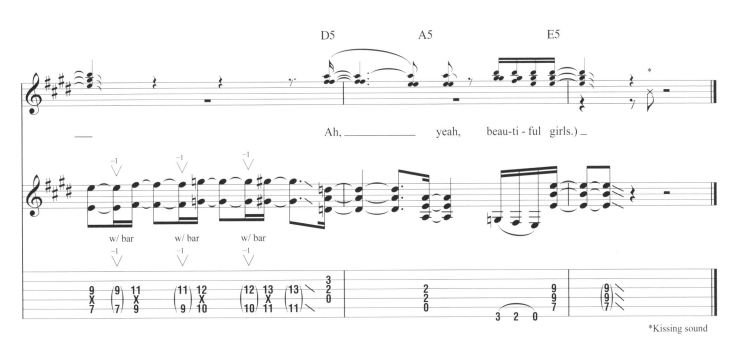

# And the Cradle Will Rock...

**Words and Music by Edward Van Halen, Alex Van Halen, Michael Anthony and David Lee Roth**

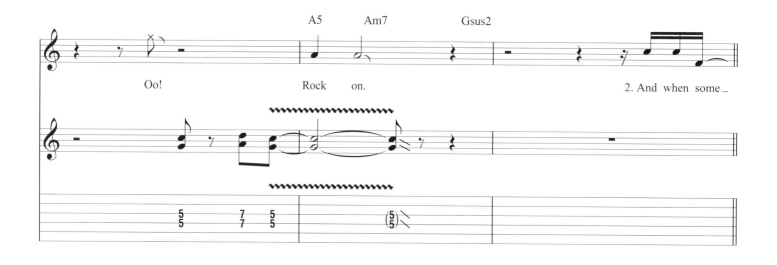

Oo!      Rock   on.        2. And when some _

**Verse**

Gtr. tacet

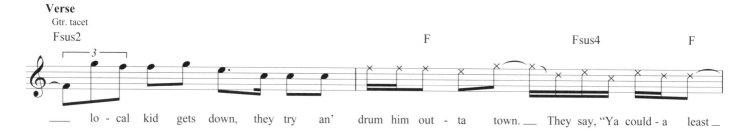

_ lo - cal kid gets down, they try an' drum him out - ta town. _ They say, "Ya could - a least _

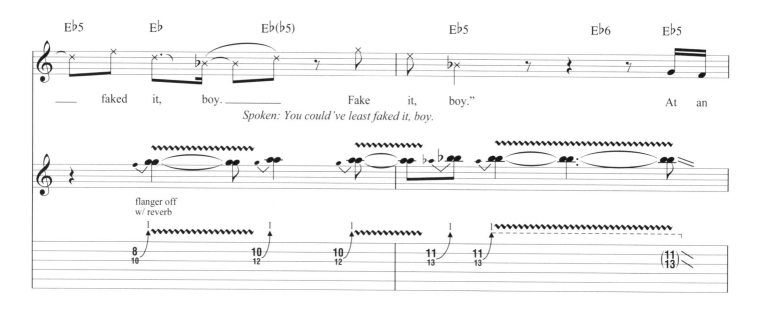

_ faked it, boy. _____ Fake it, boy."        At an

*Spoken: You could've least faked it, boy.*

flanger off
w/ reverb

Gtr. tacet

ear - ly age ___ he hits ___ the street _ and winds ___ up tied with who he meets ___ and he's

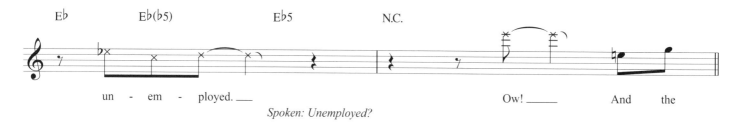

un - em - ployed. _____        Ow! _____ And the

*Spoken: Unemployed?*

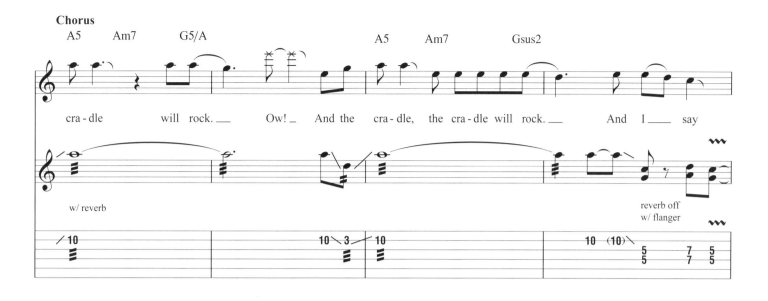

cra-dle    will rock. ___    Ow! ___ And the    cra-dle,    the cra-dle will rock. ___    And I ___ say

w/ reverb

reverb off
w/ flanger

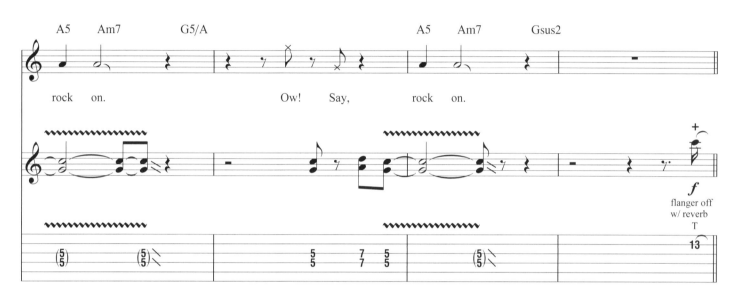

rock    on.    Ow!    Say,    rock    on.

flanger off
w/ reverb

**Guitar Solo**

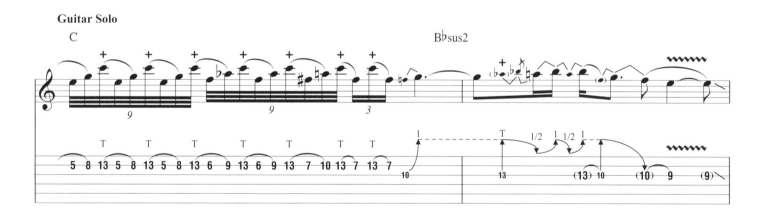

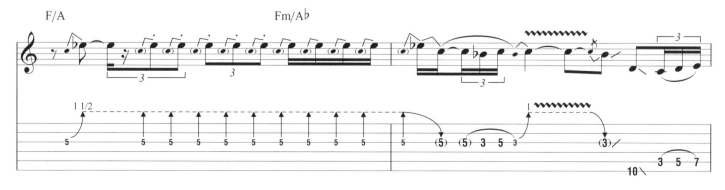

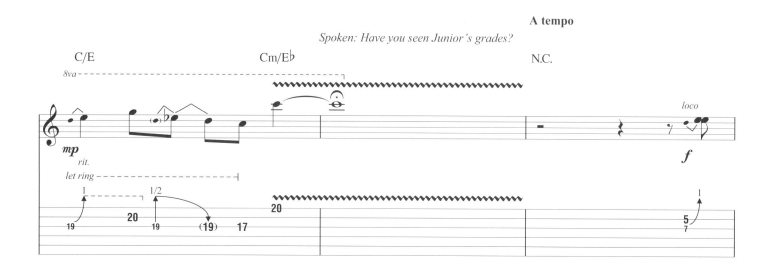

**A tempo**

*Spoken: Have you seen Junior's grades?*

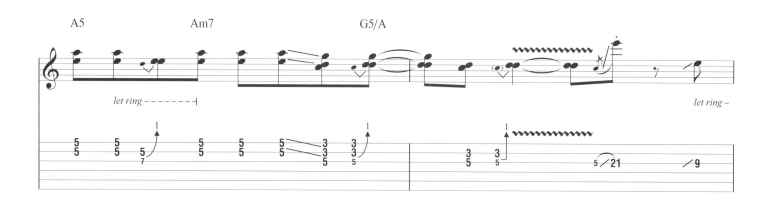

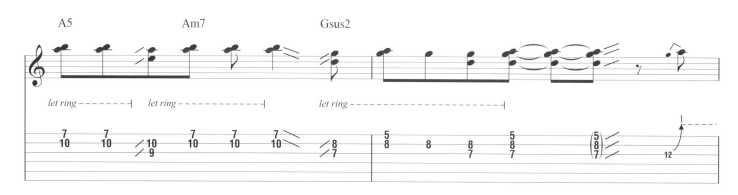

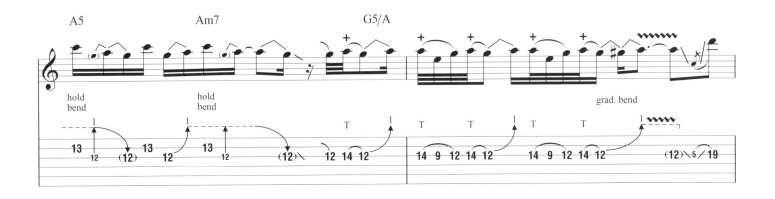

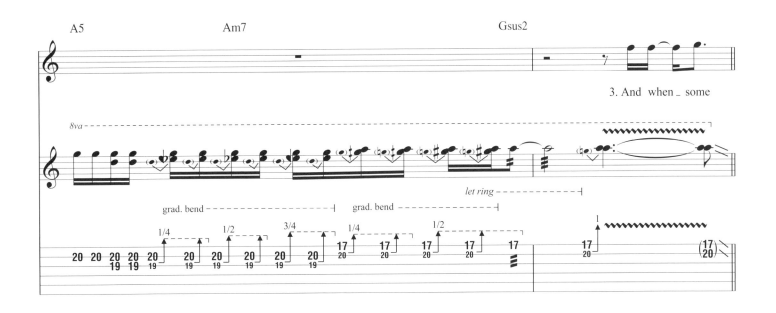

3. And when ___ some

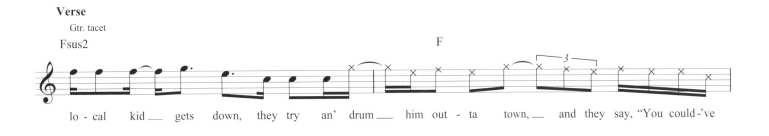

## Verse

Gtr. tacet

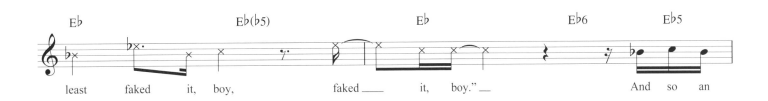

lo - cal kid ___ gets down, they try an' drum ___ him out - ta town, ___ and they say, "You could -'ve

least faked it, boy, ___ faked ___ it, boy." ___ And so an

ear - ly age, ___ he hits ___ the street ___ and winds ___ up tied ___ with who he meets ___ and he's

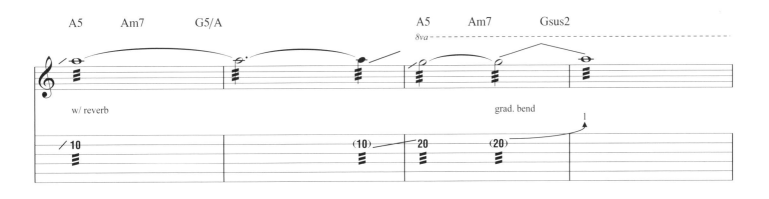

**Begin fade**

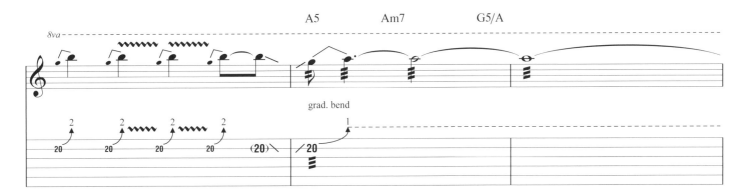

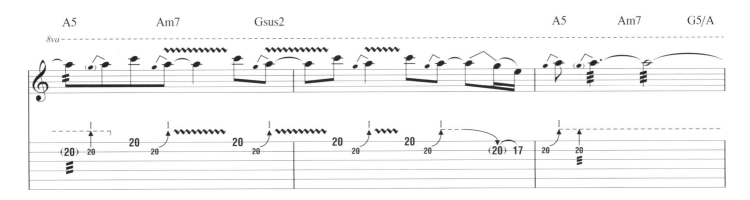

**Fade out**

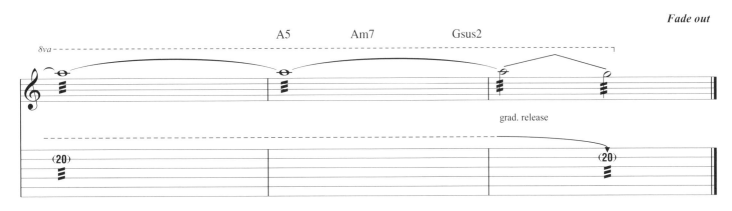

# Drop Dead Legs

### Words and Music by Edward Van Halen, Alex Van Halen and David Lee Roth

Drop D tuning:
(low to high) D-A-D-G-B-E

**Intro**
**Moderately** ♩ = 90

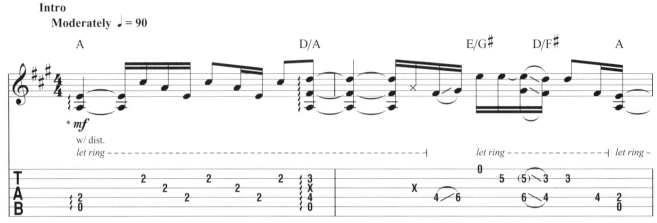

*Vol. knob set at half volume.

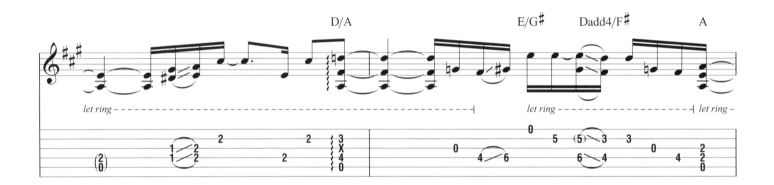

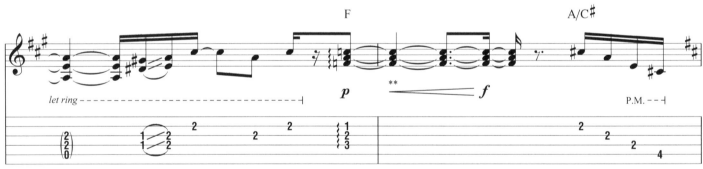

**Increase vol. knob to full volume.

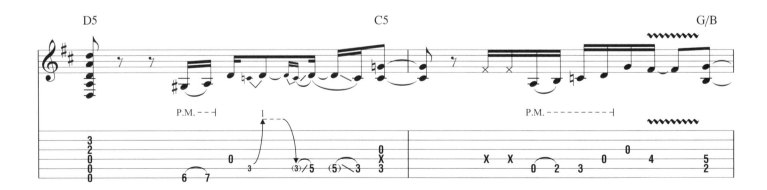

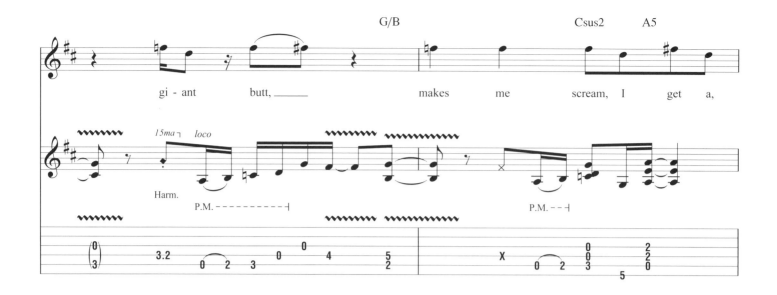

G/B       Csus2    A5

gi - ant butt, _____ makes me scream, I get a,

D5            C5           G/B

nuh, nuh, noth - in' but the shakes o - ver you. _____ Drop
(Drop dead legs.)

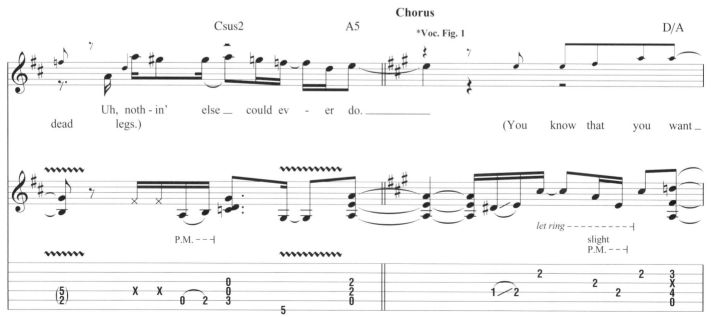

**Chorus**

Csus2     A5    *Voc. Fig. 1            D/A

Uh, noth - in' else _ could ev - er do. _____ (You know that you want _
dead legs.)

*Refers to upstemmed part only.

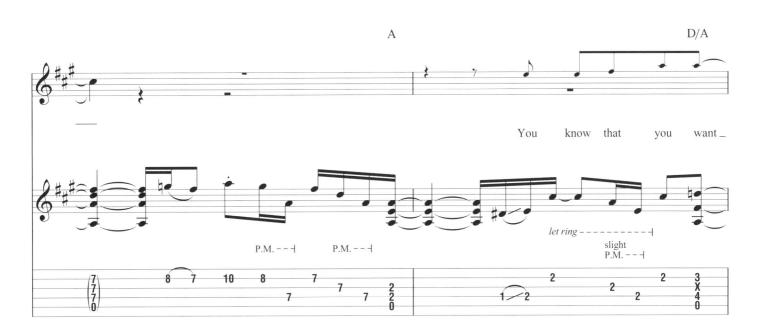

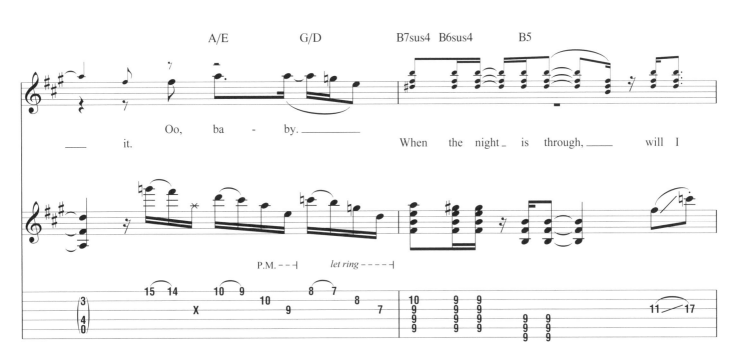

**Chorus**
Bkgd. Voc.: w/ Voc. Fig. 1

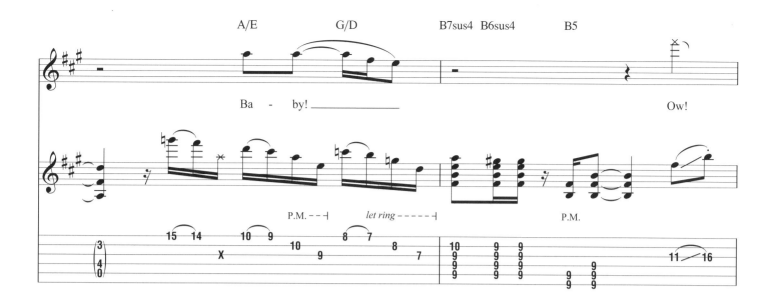

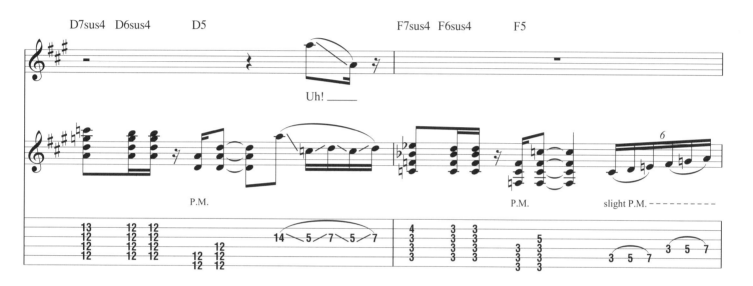

*Key signature denotes D Mixolydian.

**Adds pitch one octave below notes played.

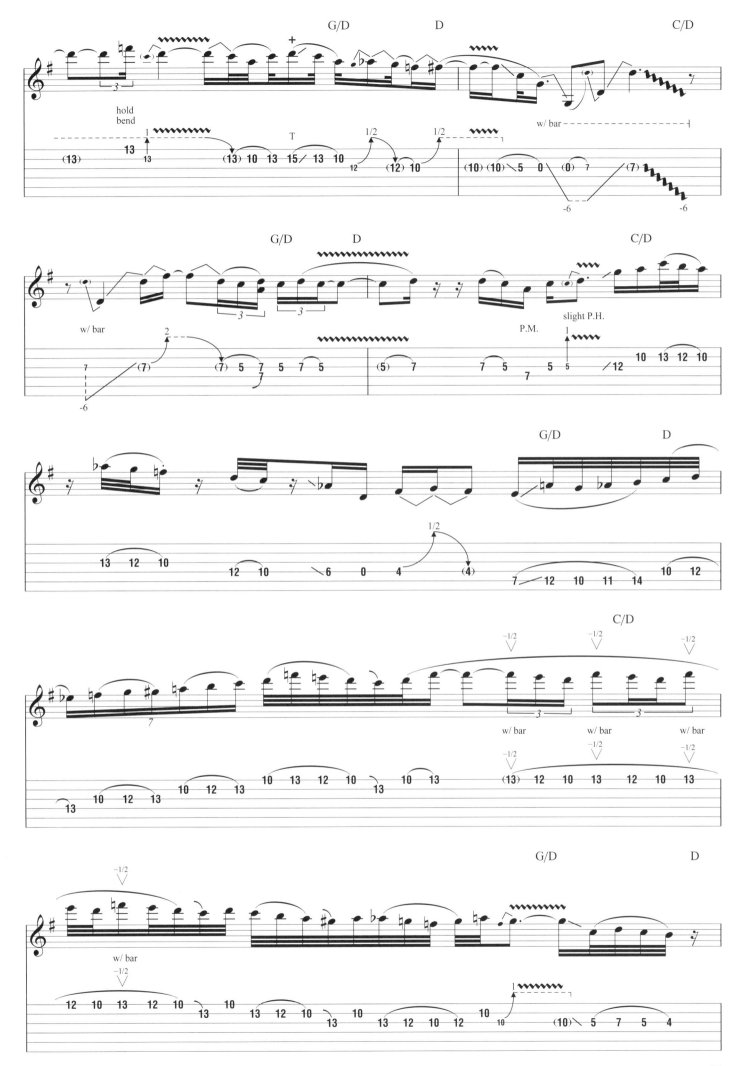

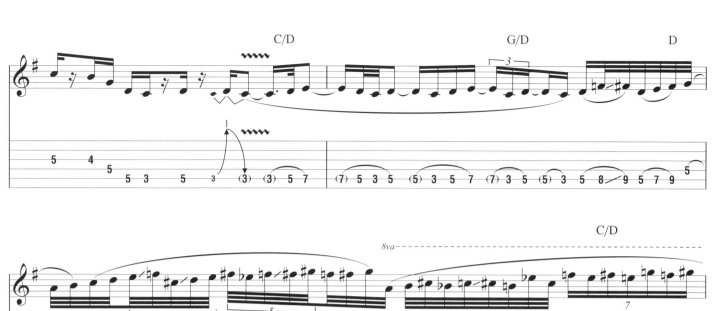

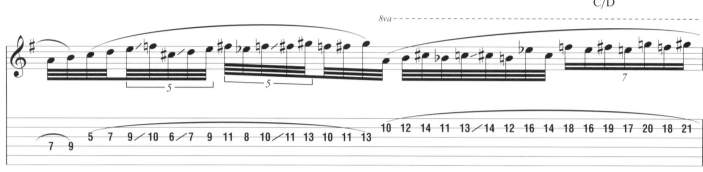

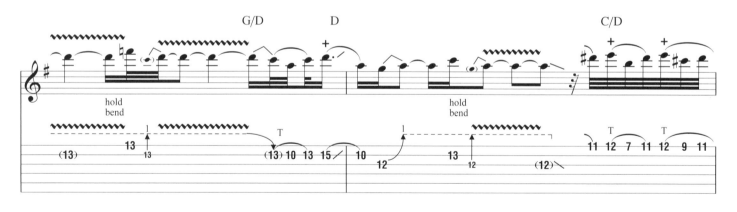

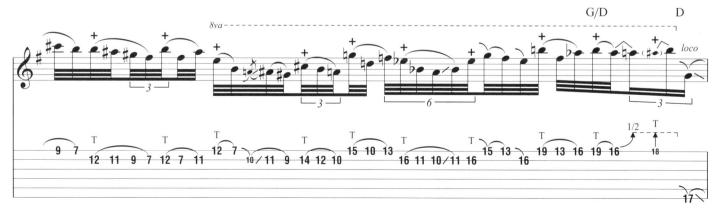

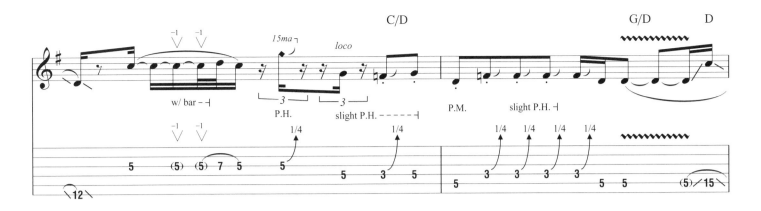

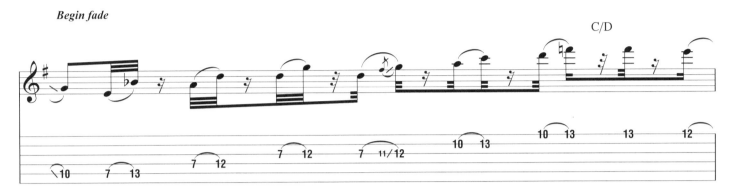

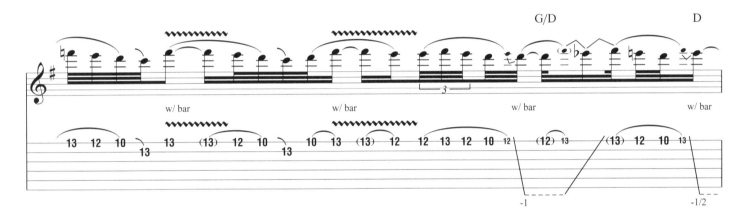

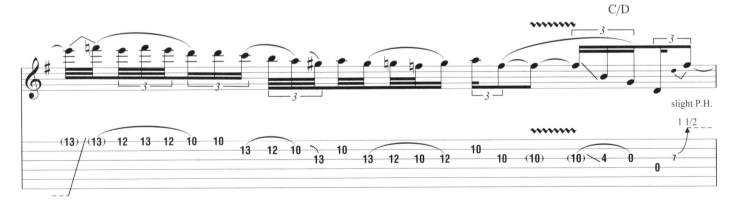

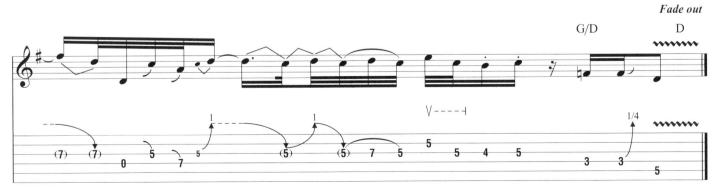

# Hot for Teacher

**Words and Music by Edward Van Halen, Alex Van Halen and David Lee Roth**

*Chord symbols reflect overall harmony.

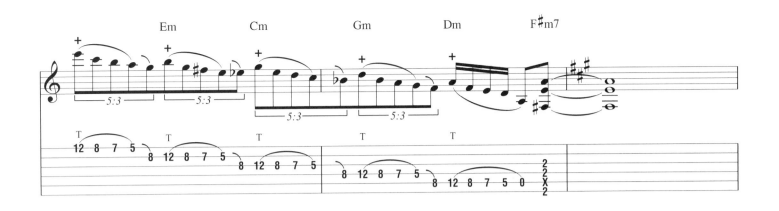

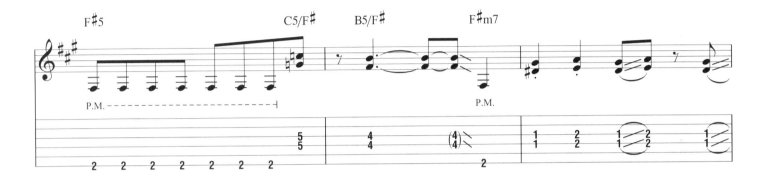

*Thumb on 6th string.

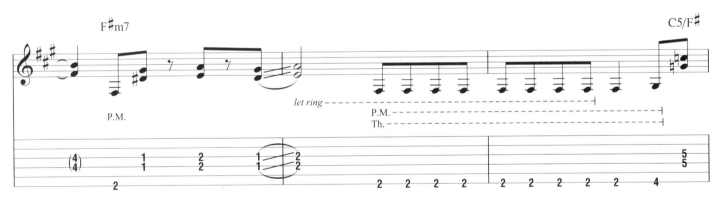

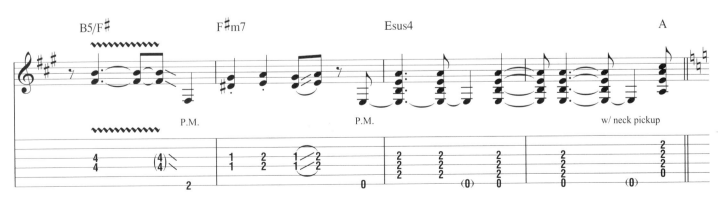

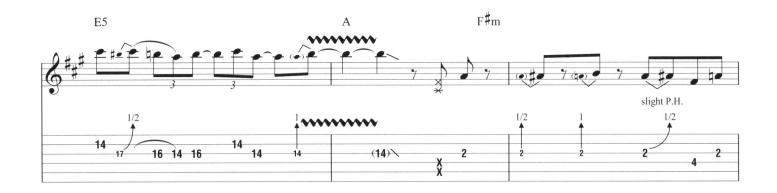

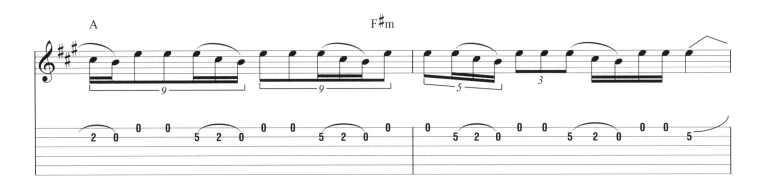

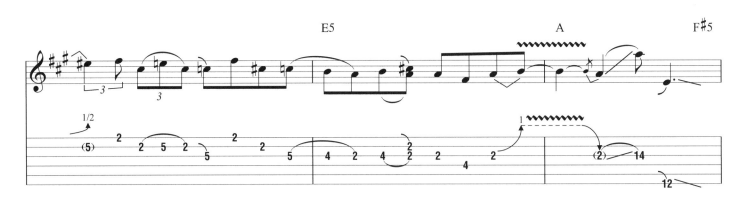

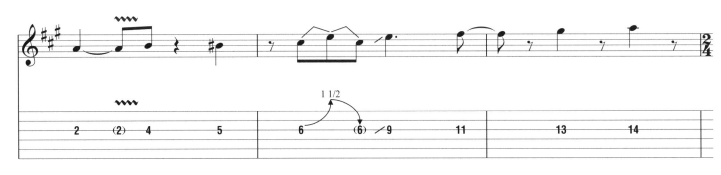

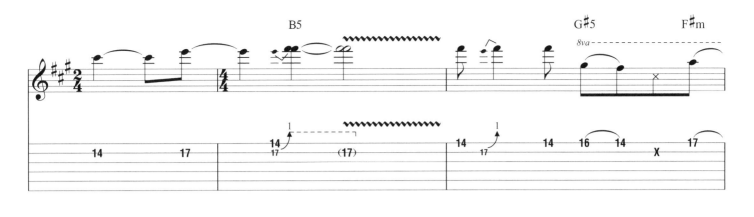

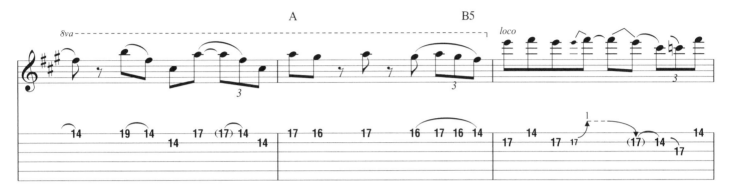

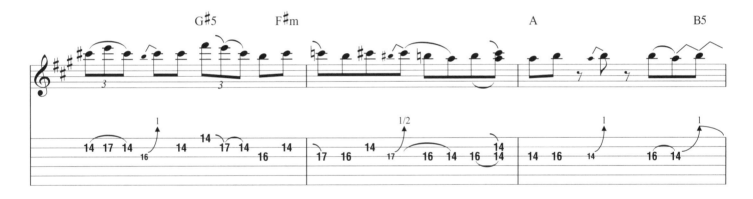

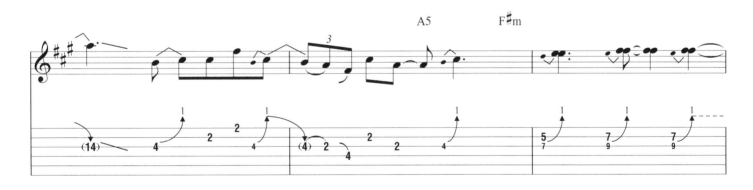

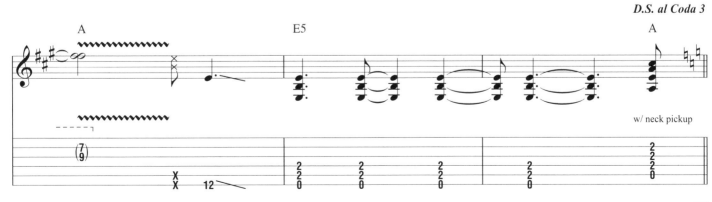

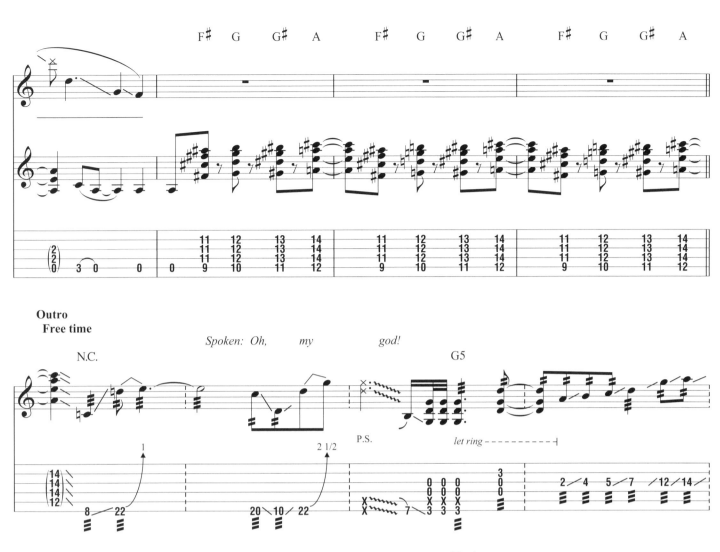

F# G G# A   F# G G# A   F# G G# A

**Outro**
**Free time**

*Spoken: Oh,   my   god!*

N.C.

G5

P.S.

*let ring* - - - - - - - - - - -

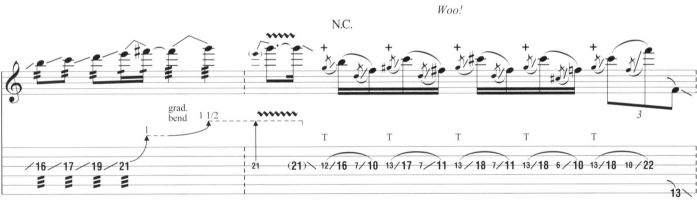

*Woo!*

N.C.

grad.
bend

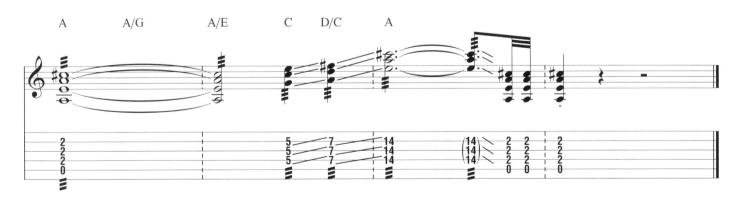

A   A/G   A/E   C   D/C   A

*Additional Lyrics*

2. I heard about your lessons, but lessons are so cold.
   I know about this school.
   Little girl from Cherry Lawn, how can you be so bold?
   How did you know that golden rule?

# Jamie's Cryin'

**Words and Music by Edward Van Halen, Alex Van Halen, Michael Anthony and David Lee Roth**

Tune down 1/2 step:
(low to high) Eb-Ab-Db-Gb-Bb-Eb

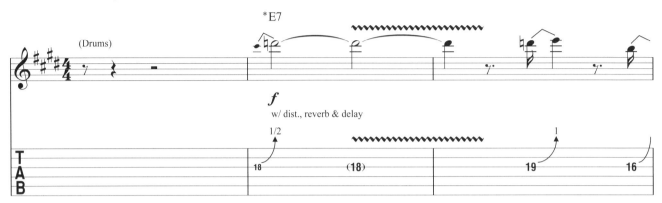

*Chord symbols reflect implied harmony.

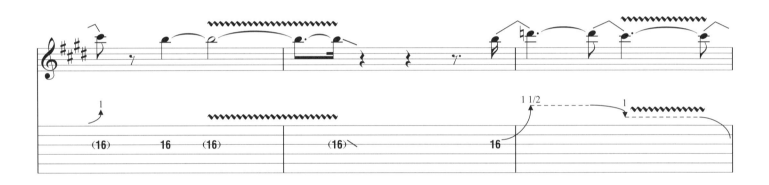

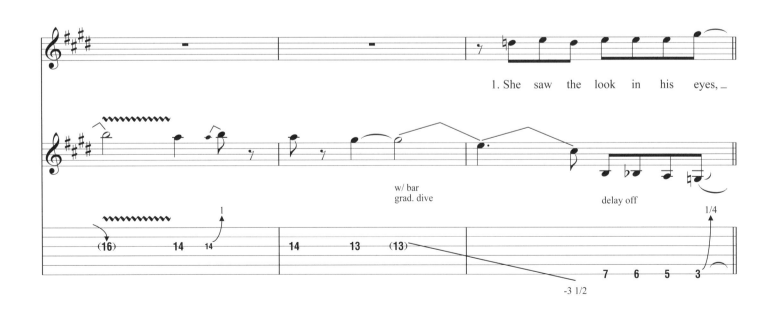

61

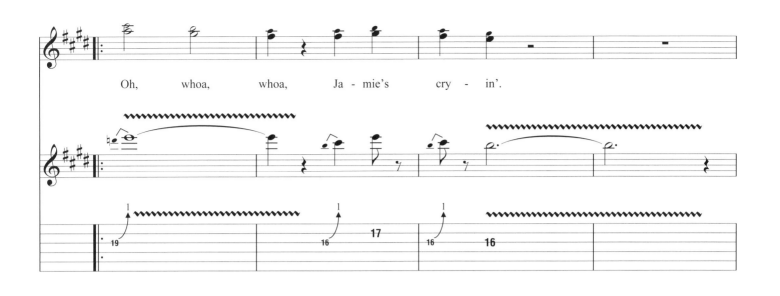

Oh, whoa, whoa, Ja - mie's cry - in'.

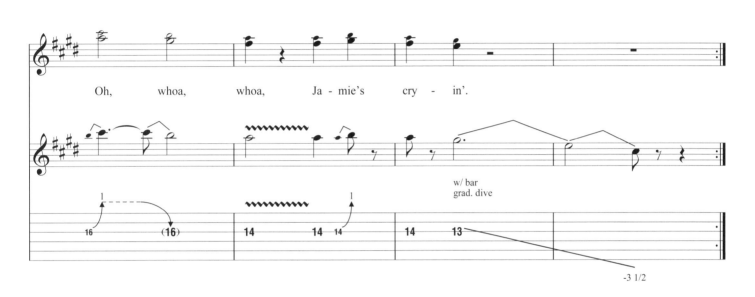

Oh, whoa, whoa, Ja - mie's cry - in'.

w/ bar
grad. dive

-3 1/2

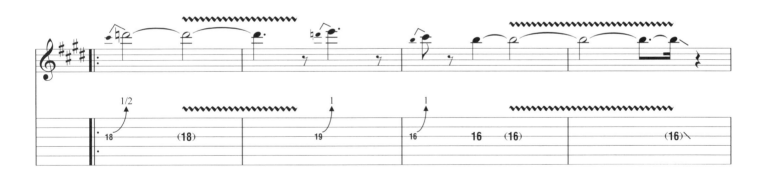

*Repeat and fade*

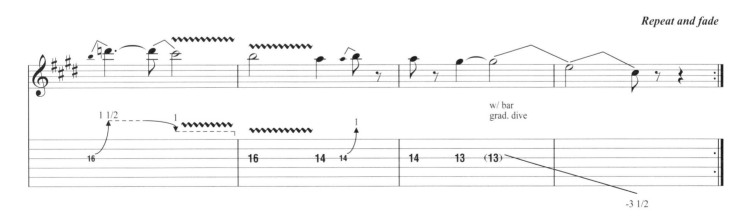

w/ bar
grad. dive

-3 1/2

# Mean Street

**Words and Music by Edward Van Halen, Alex Van Halen, Michael Anthony and David Lee Roth**

Tune down 1/2 step:
(low to high) E♭-A♭-D♭-G♭-B♭-E♭

**Intro**
**Moderately fast** ♩ = 132

N.C.

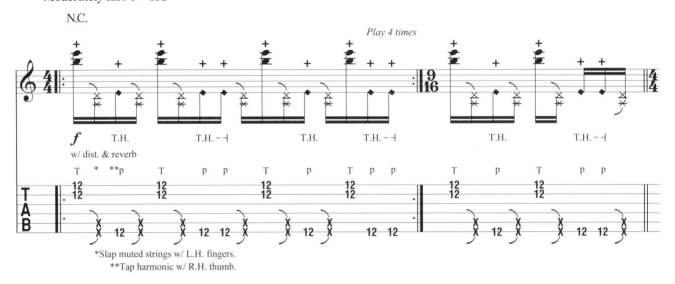

*Slap muted strings w/ L.H. fingers.
**Tap harmonic w/ R.H. thumb.

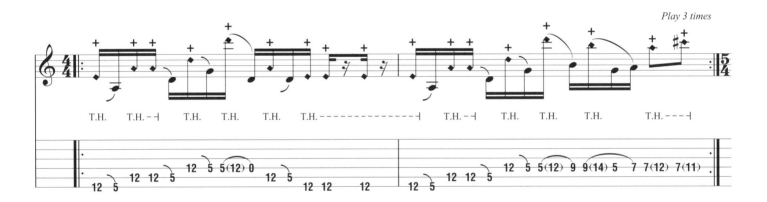

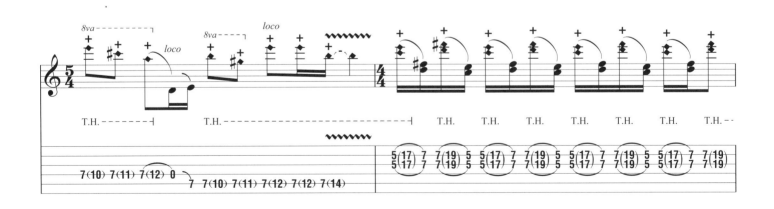

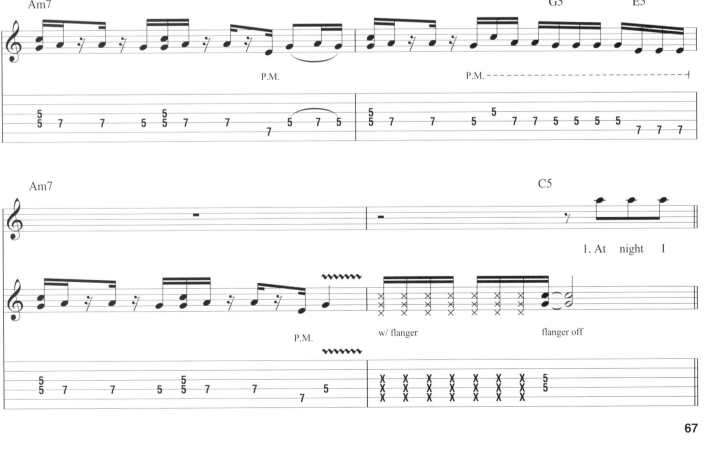

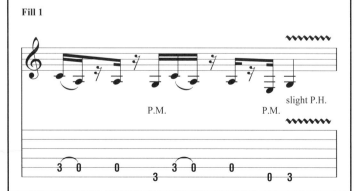

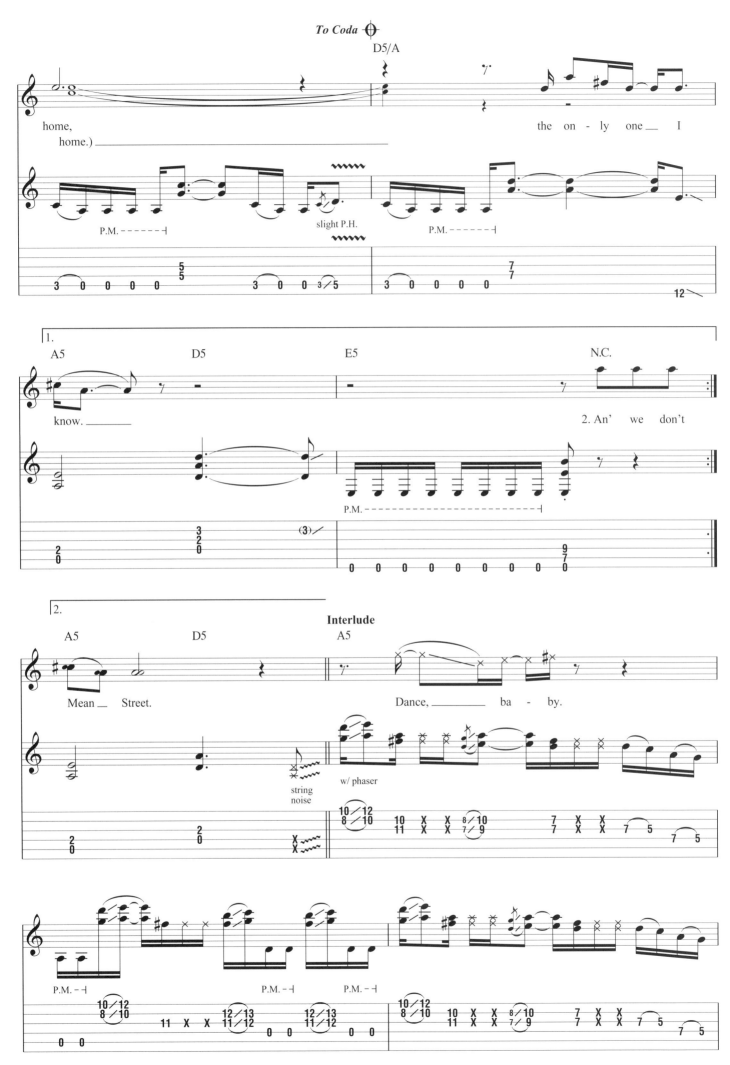

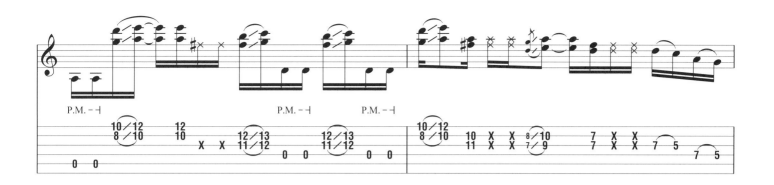

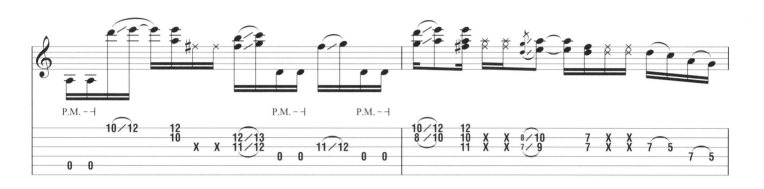

**Guitar Solo**

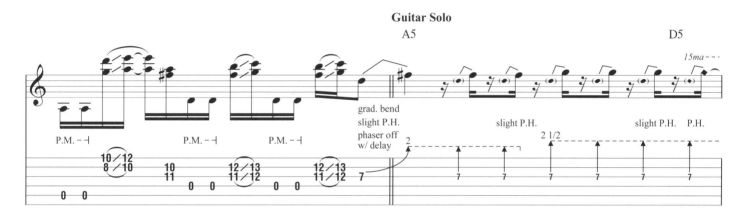

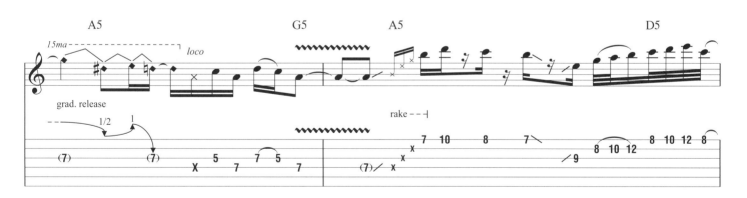

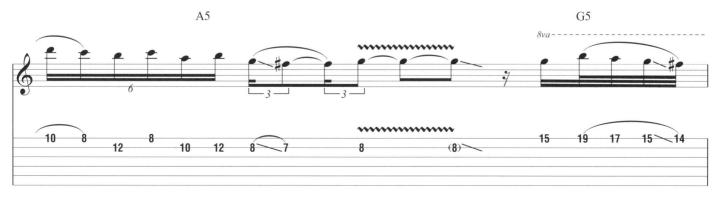

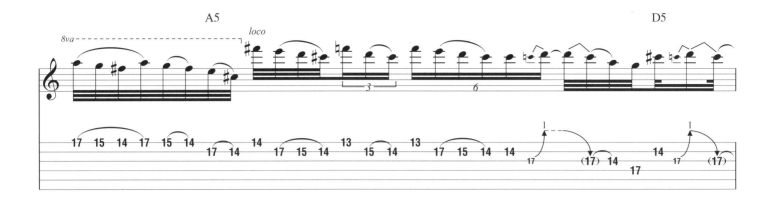

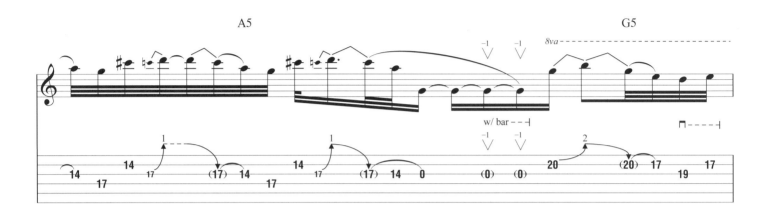

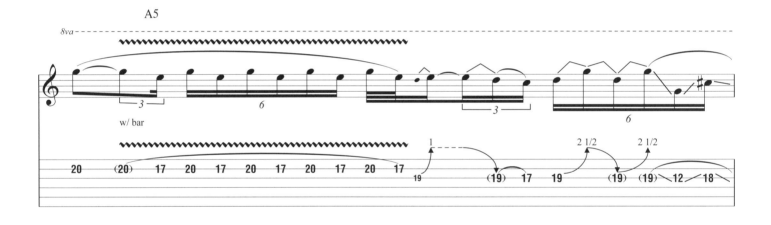

**D.S. al Coda**

$\oplus$ **Coda**

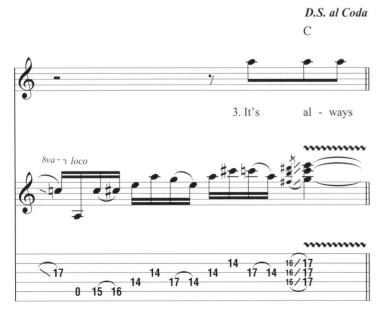

3. It's al - ways

on - ly one __ I

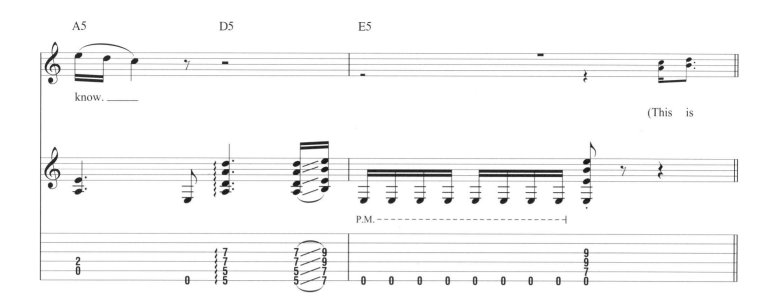

A5   D5   E5

know. _____

(This is

**Bridge**

Am7   D/A

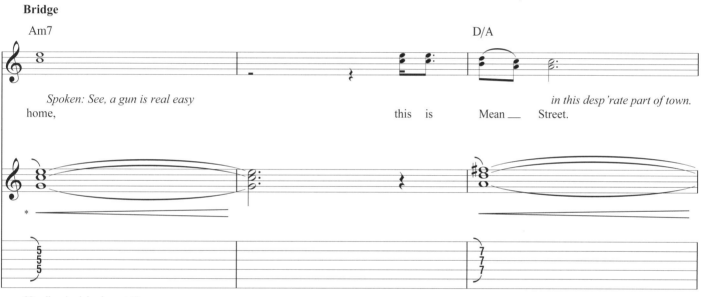

*Spoken: See, a gun is real easy*

home,

this is   Mean __ Street.

*in this desp'rate part of town.*

*Swells w/ vol. knob, next 12 meas.

Am7

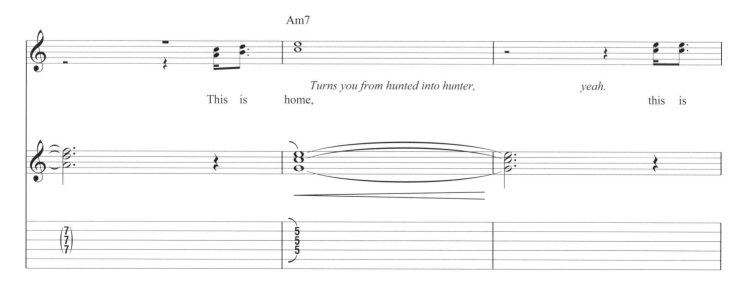

*Turns you from hunted into hunter,*

This is   home,

*yeah.*

this is

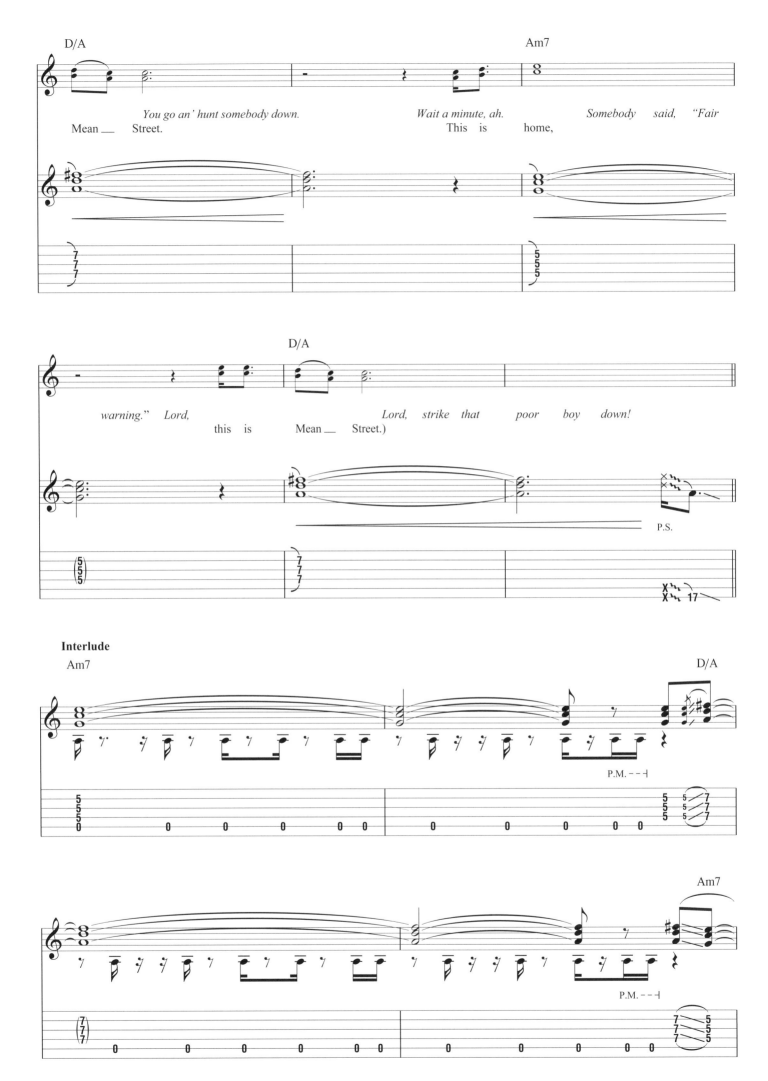

D/A

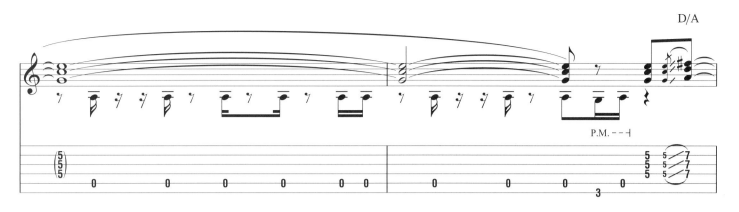

Am7

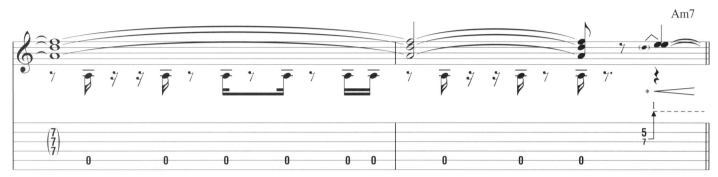

*Swell w/ vol. knob.

**Outro-Guitar Solo**

Am7                                                                 D/A

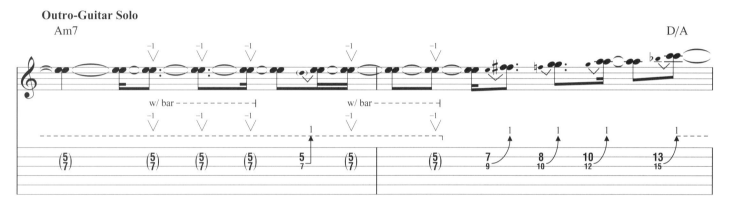

Am7

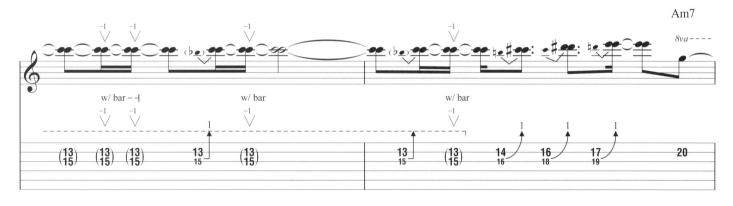

D/A

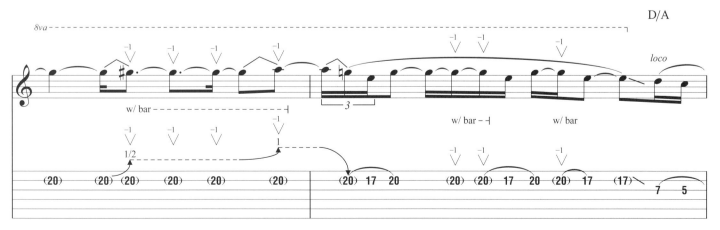

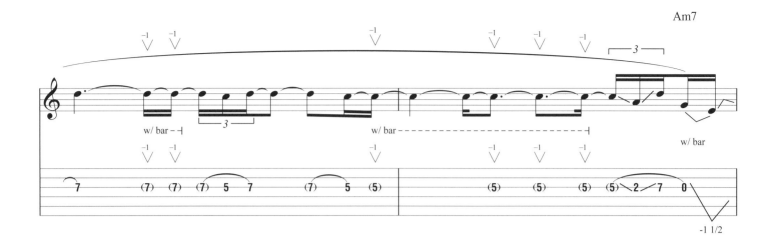

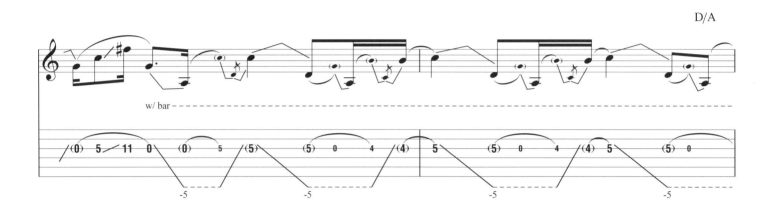

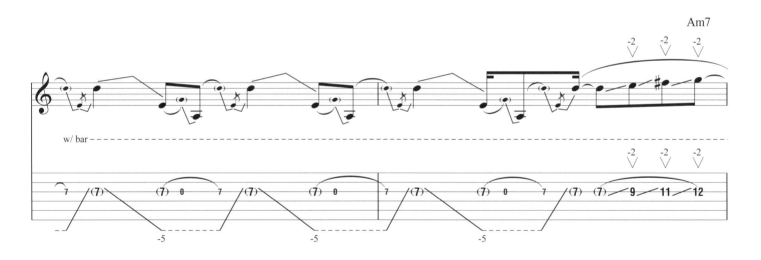

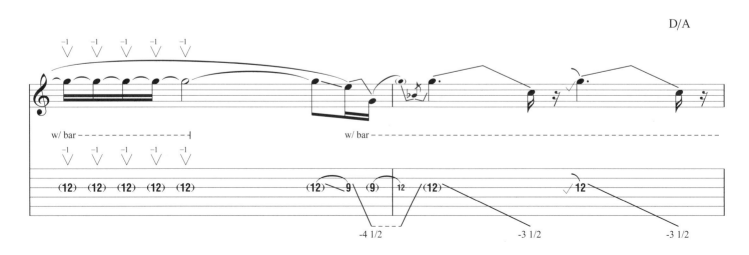

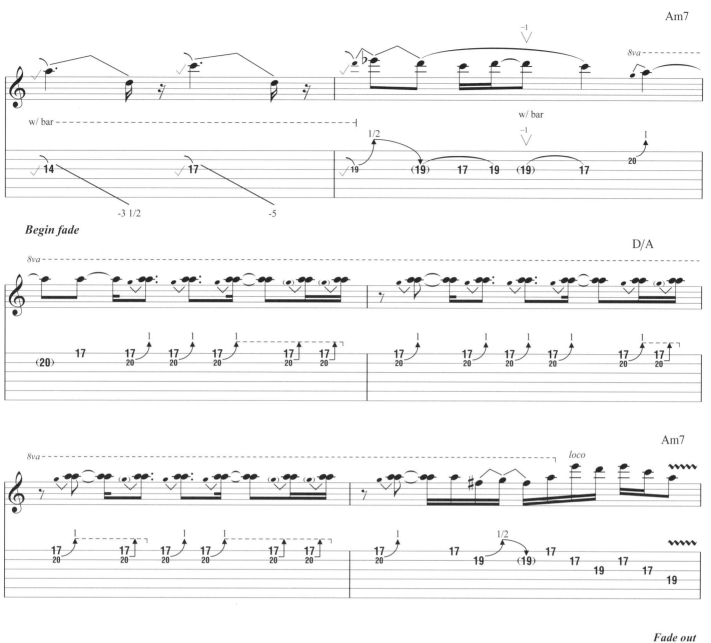

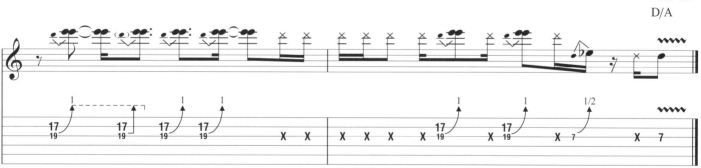

*Additional Lyrics*

2. An' we don't worry 'bout tomorrow 'cause we're sick of these four walls.
   Now, what you think is nothin' might be somethin' after all.
   Now, you know this ain't no through street. The end is dead ahead.
   The poor folks play for keeps down here. They're the living dead.

*Chorus*   Come on down, ah, huh, down to Mean Street.
   They're dancin' now, look, out on Mean Street.

3. It's always here and now, my friend. It ain't once upon a time.
   It's all over but the shouting. I come to take what's mine.
   We're searchin' for the latest thing, a break in this routine.
   Talkin' some new kicks, ones like you ain't never seen.

# Somebody Get Me a Doctor

**Words and Music by Edward Van Halen, Alex Van Halen, Michael Anthony and David Lee Roth**

Tune down 1/2 step:
(low to high) E♭-A♭-D♭-G♭-B♭-E♭

**Intro**
**Moderately** ♩ = 130

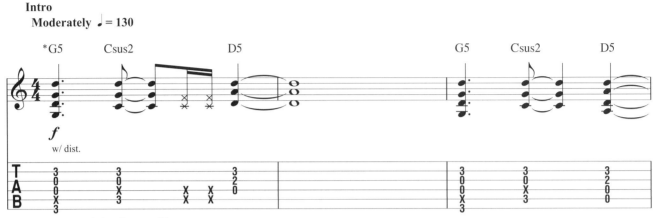

*Chord symbols reflect overall harmony.

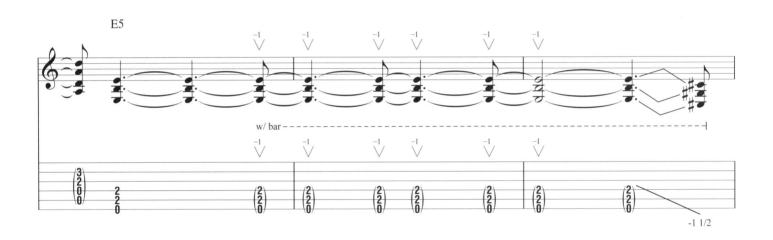

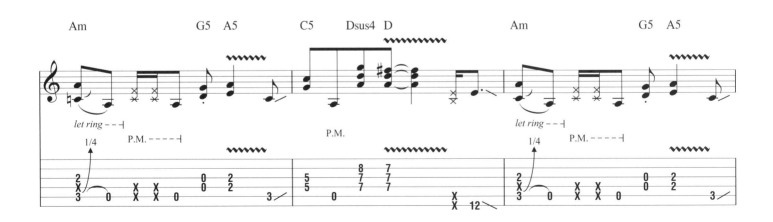

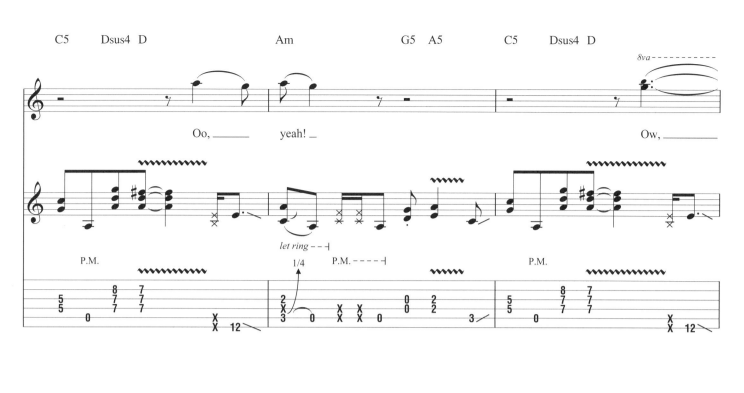

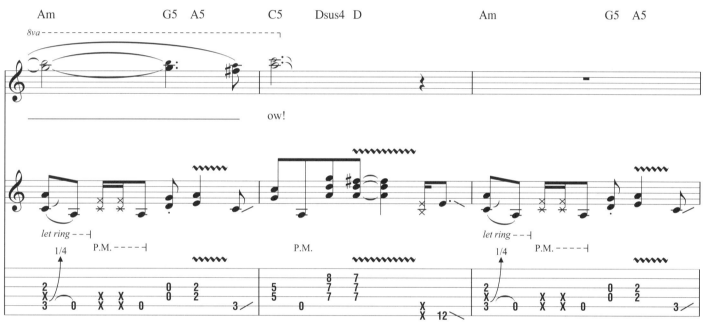

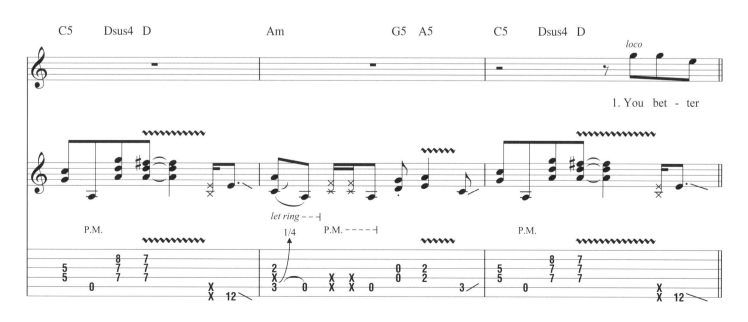

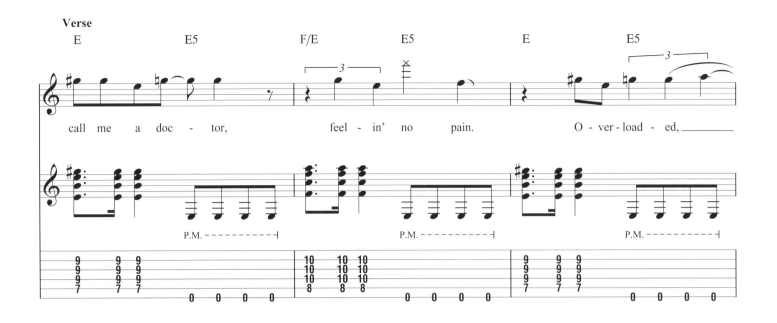

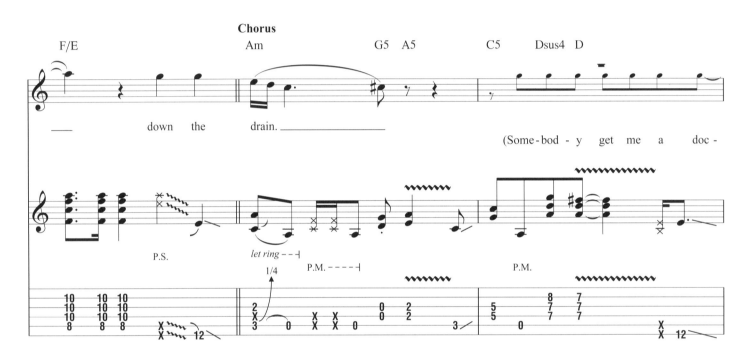

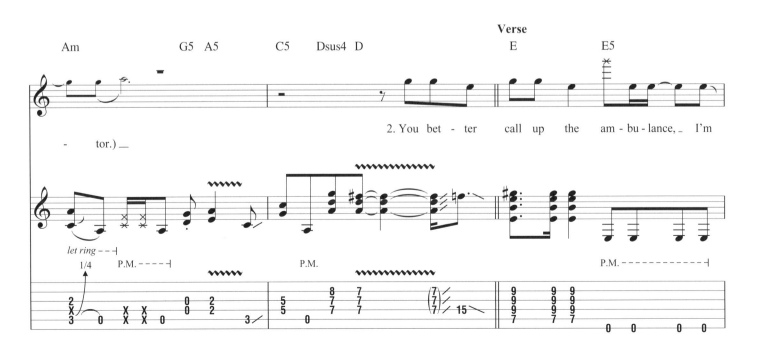

deep in shock. _____ O - ver - load - ed, ba - by, I can _____ hard - ly

**Chorus**

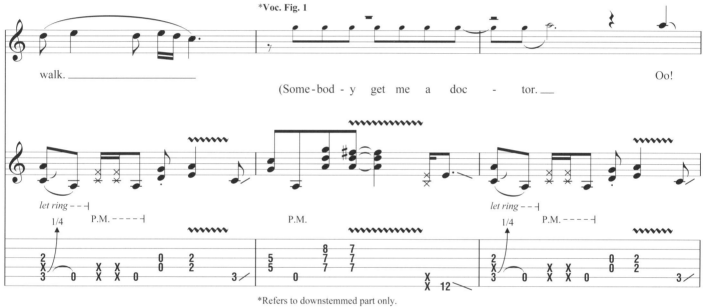

walk. _____ (Some - bod - y get me a doc - tor. ___) Oo!

*Refers to downstemmed part only.

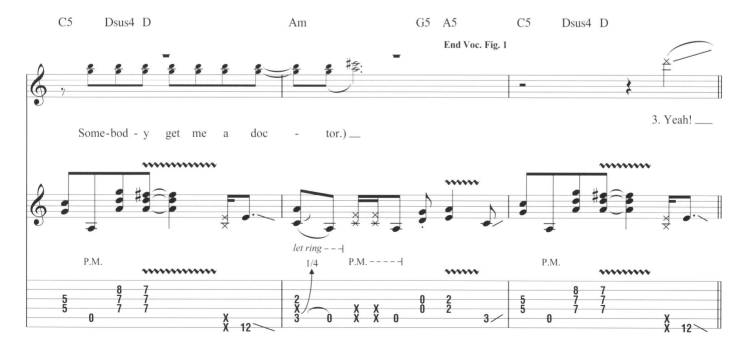

Some - bod - y get me a doc - tor.) ___ 3. Yeah! ___

**Verse**

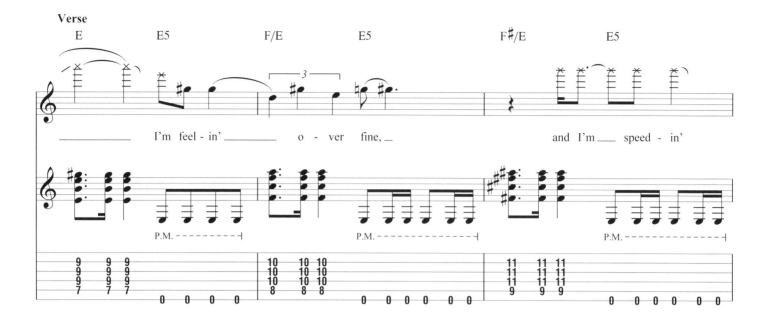

_I'm feel-in'_ _____ _o - ver fine,_ _____ _and I'm_ ___ _speed - in'_

**Interlude**

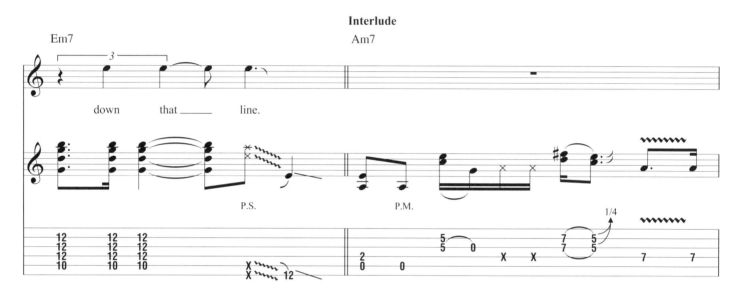

_down_ _that_ _____ _line._

P.S.    P.M.

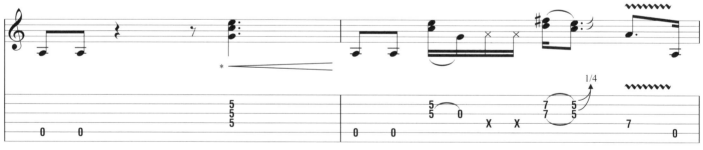

*Swells w/ vol. knob throughout.

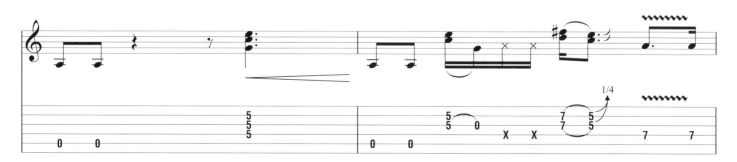

Woo, woo! _____

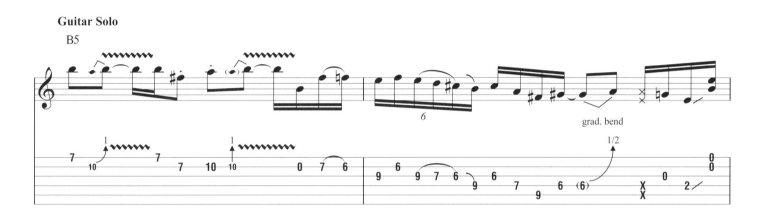

grad. bend

**Guitar Solo**

B5

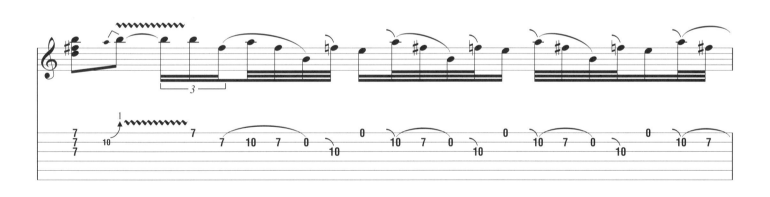

grad. bend

G5

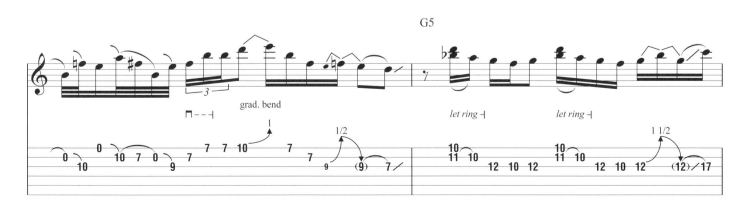

grad. bend

*let ring* ⌐    *let ring* ⌐

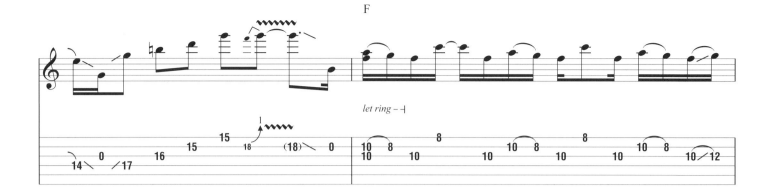

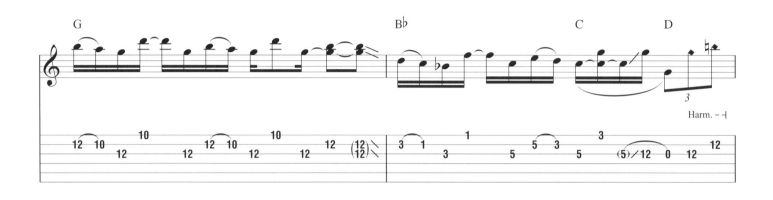

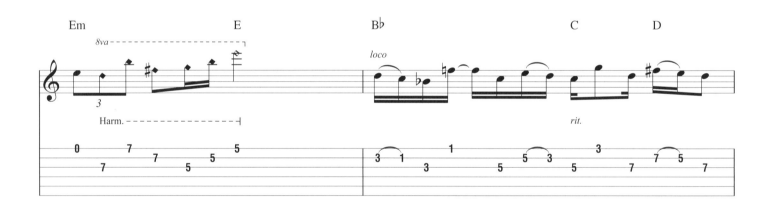

**Free time**

**A tempo**

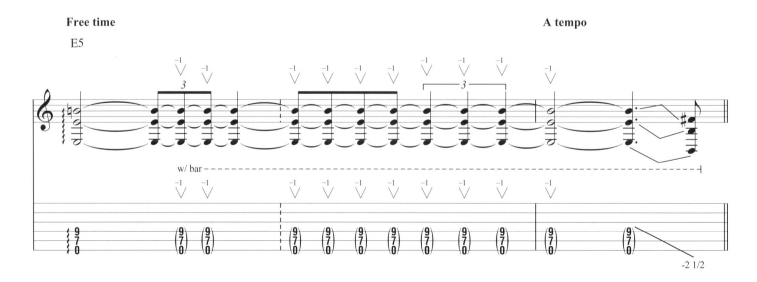

## Interlude

*Slide R.H. from bridge toward neck while lightly touching strings w/ palm edge, sounding random harmonics.

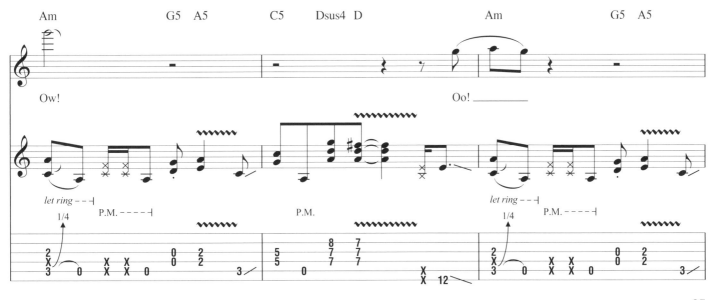

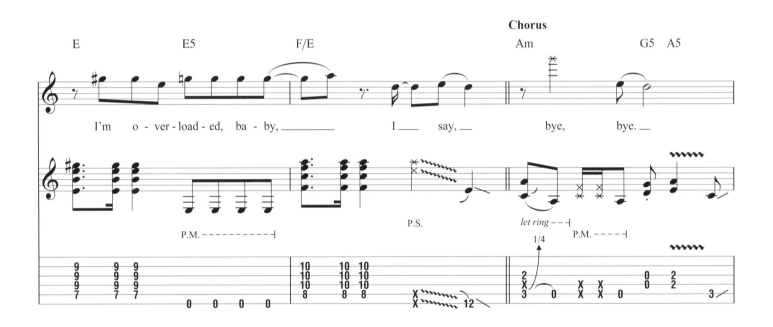

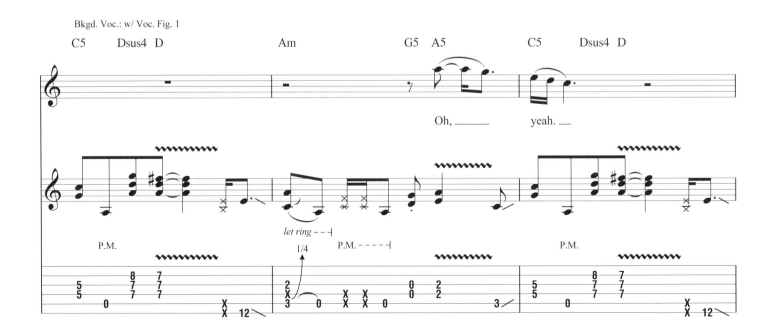

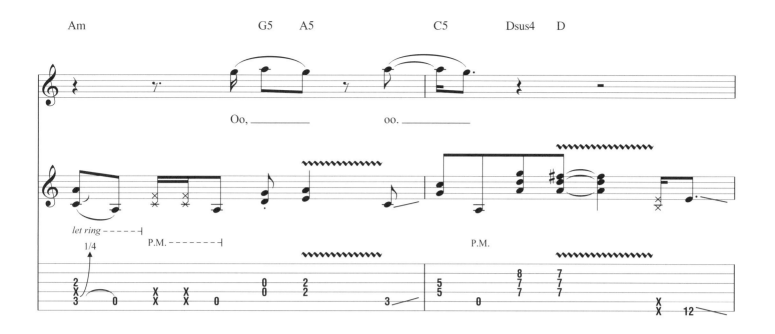

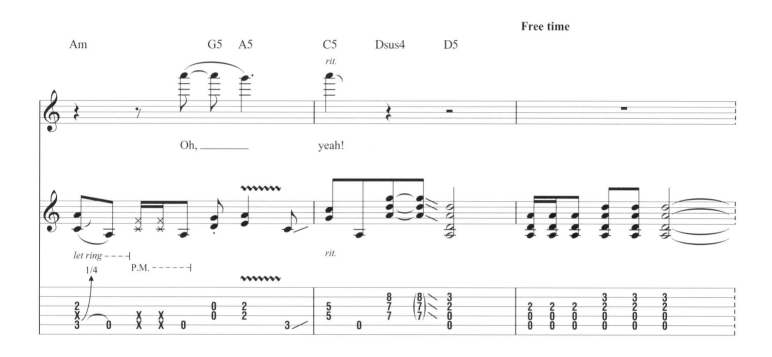

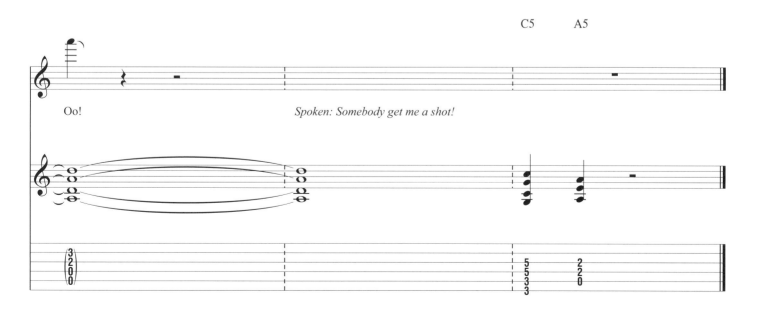

# HAL•LEONARD GUITAR PLAY-ALONG

This series will help you play your favorite songs quickly and easily. Just follow the tab and listen to the CD to the hear how the guitar should sound, and then play along using the separate backing tracks. Mac or PC users can also slow down the tempo without changing pitch by using the CD in their computer. The melody and lyrics are included in the book so that you can sing or simply follow along.

**INCLUDES TAB**

**Complete song lists available online.**

*Prices, contents, and availability subject to change without notice.*

HAL•LEONARD® CORPORATION
7777 W. BLUEMOUND RD. P.O. BOX 13819 MILWAUKEE, WI 53213

www.halleonard.com

0314